PHOTOGRAPHER

MW00490956

Weird, Wild, and Wonderful
Connecticut

Christina E. Cole

AMERICA
THROUGH TIME®
ADDING COLOR TO AMERICAN HISTORY

Please note that some historical materials may contain offensive content.

America Through time is an imprint of Fonthill Media LLC
www.through-time.com
office@through-time.com

Published by Arcadia Publishing by arrangement with Fonthill Media LLC
For all general information, please contact Arcadia Publishing:
Telephone: 843-853-2070
Fax: 843-853-0044
E-mail: sales@arcadiapublishing.com
For customer service and orders:
Toll-Free 1-888-313-2665

www.arcadiapublishing.com

First published 2022

Copyright © Christina E. Cole 2022

ISBN 978-1-63499-402-6

Typeset in Gotham Book
Printed and bound in England

Contents

Acknowledgments

Thank you to all the residents of Connecticut who have given the time of day to my wide-eyed wonderment of their beautiful state, endured my endless questions from flowers to porcupines, and did not throw me out of their yard as I snapped anything and everything odd.

Thank you to those who rode along and humored me when I excitedly asked them to pull over. Mostly, to my wonderful boyfriend, who drove, trekked through tick infested woods, sat through hours of birding and the personalities associated with it, and had one foot on the gas not knowing if someone was going to come hollering at the trespassers: thank you, David Graham, for giving up your hours to my passion. You are good company and I love you.

Lastly, thank you to my editors and publishers at Fonthill Media for opportunity to put my photography and words into books through *Photographer's America*.

Foreword

What are the marks and measures of the character of the world around us? Ask any number of people, and you'll get any number of answers. The multitudinous nature of an individual's experience is quite hard to pin down to a short, concise description. So, we struggle to whittle these concepts down to manageable ideas and phrases, if for nothing else than relaying our experience to the closest level of understanding possible. It is an involving and evolving journey, sociologically and psychologically, for the whole and the individual. And without the experiences of the individual, the amalgamation of the entity would have no meaning.

If Christina's perspective were any easier to distill, this entire rambling of mine would be unnecessary. I have the unique perspective of knowing and observing her and her craft on a day-to-day basis, sometimes minute to minute. This knowledge still gives me only a tiny understanding of what truly goes on in her swirling construction of thoughts. They are deep and wide, and the simplistic can become complicated, and the complicated becomes simple. It's a process of bringing the internal to the external. Her method of projecting, through photography, is definitely one of the easiest methods to access. Without explanation, we can examine and interpret what we believe are her thoughts and intentions. But all we can truly see is our surface understanding, for our minds can't completely realize every breath, camera click, or sense of interest and wonder that underlies her decisions for every photo she produces. She is like all of us. She is also unlike any of us. But her photography and her mind are the same.

They are wild.
They are weird.
They are wonderful.

David Graham

Introduction

Alone is not necessarily the absence of others but the ability to be comfortable in and enjoy one's own company. When I hold a camera and look through the viewfinder, everything else disappears and I am one with what I see. The buzz of the world ceases to exist. Conditions may not always be perfect, light is not always available, and a picture is not always what you saw, but the ability to lose oneself in the moment is always worth the action. An explorer's eyes are never closed. I constantly look, access, think, plan, and act, and my mind never stops. I appreciate everything I see and hope to bring it to people the way I saw it. Of course, the viewer's interpretations are their own, but that is the art of the photograph.

Life should not be a journey to the grave with the intention of arriving safely in a pretty and well-preserved body, but rather to skid in broadside in a cloud of smoke, thoroughly used up, totally worn out, and loudly proclaiming, "Wow! What a ride!"

Hunter S. Thompson

1

The Dinosaurs

Connecticut might be the smallest state, but it once housed our continent's most prominent inhabitants, dinosaurs. Dilophosauraus was one dinosaur that walked our soil. This species is designated as Connecticut's state dinosaur. Tracks from this giant of the Jurassic era were discovered in the mid-60s by a bulldozer operator. Dilophosauraus was close to twenty-three feet in length and weighed upwards of 880 pounds. The animal's head was large, ending in a narrow snout and adorned with two longitudinal arched crests. Dilophosaurus is best known for its depiction in Michael Crichton's novel and the film by Steven Spielberg, *Jurassic Park.* The film exaggerated the dinosaur to spit venom and gave it an expanding independently shaking neck frill to make it even more menacing.

Connecticut State prides itself on its dinosaur trail. The points of interest of these trails are:

- East Windsor Academy Museum, East Windsor
- Old Town Hall Museum, Enfield
- Bruce Museum, Greenwich
- Connecticut Science Center, Hartford
- Powder Hill Dinosaur Park, Middlefield
- Joe Webb Peoples Museum, Middletown
- The Dinosaur Place at Nature's Art Village, Montville
- Wells Dinosaur Haven, Montville
- Othniel Charles Marsh House, New Haven
- Yale Peabody Museum, New Haven
- Dinosaur State Park, Rocky Hill
- The Children's Museum, West Hartford
- Eubrontes Fossil Hunt, Windsor

There are three prominent attractions on the path. The first of these attractions is the Dinosaur State Park, located in Rocky Hill, Connecticut. It houses one of the largest dinosaur track sites in North America. In addition to the 200-million-year-old tracks, the geodesic domed museum also presents a bird's-eye view of the preserved Mesozoic flood plain, interactive exhibits, dioramas of the Triassic, and Jurassic environments, and a variety of fossils. Outside, you will find two miles of trails and approximately 250 living representatives of the plant families that appeared in the age of dinosaurs.

The Dinosaur Place, located in Oakdale, is a sixty-acre nature park with a mile-and-a-half of hiking trails and over fifty life-sized dinosaurs. Animatronic dinosaurs are around every corner, next to an erupting volcano, and deep in caves throughout the property. The exhibit has successfully added a dinosaur every year for twenty years, ensuring visitors always see something exciting and new.

The Peabody Museum of Natural History's Great Hall of Dinosaurs centers on a mounted Brontosaurus. Trailing the top of the room is the masterpiece by Rudolph Zallinger, "The Age of Reptiles." Encased in the outer edges of the museum's corridors are many reticulated skeletons showcasing all life from these fascinating periods. From petrified wood, toothed birds, fossil footprints, crinoids, and the largest turtle species, the great hall has been wowing visitors since 1926.

The T-Rex to the entrance of the Dinosaur Place.

Dilophosaurus, the dinosaur that made the tracks on display at the Dinosaur Museum.

Left: Pterosaurs, with hollow bones making them lightweight, lived from the late Triassic Period through the end of the Cretaceous Period.

Below: Deinonychus, or the Velociraptor, inspired Michael Crichton's *Jurassic Park*. Deinonychus means "terrible claw."

Deinonychus, paleontologist John Ostrum's fleet-footed, agile and predacious discovery, articulated for the museum.

Ceratopsian skulls in the Great Hall of the Peabody Museum.

A Brontosaurus and Rudolph Zallinger's mural, "The Age of Reptiles."

Bird's-eye view of the preserved Mesozoic floodplain covered with tracks at the Dinosaur Museum.

2

The Birds and Conservation

Moving on to today's dinosaurs, one of the many efforts in bettering our state not only comes from the numerous outdoor sanctuaries, open spaces, and land preservation areas but the continued marriage of efforts between like-minded organizations to work together on their goals. The Connecticut Audubon and DEEP are at the forefront of scores of avian conservation efforts, and a good deal of protection operations stand out. However, one shines when safeguarding our feathered friends: A Place Called Hope.

A Place Called Hope

A Place Called Hope (APCH), situated in Killingworth, is a non-profit bird of prey reha-bilitation center. The center's goal is to rehab and release birds into the wild whenever possible. From fallen nestlings to car strikes, their team makes every effort to reintroduce the birds back into their natural habitat. When they are not releasable, APCH is federally permitted to house them on-site for education purposes. Through this educational series, they can teach people about raptors, their impact on our environment, how they are our natural pest control, and why we should not use rodenticides, pesticides, or lead anything when it comes to hunting. When we offset the balance between birds of prey and nature, we set a cycle in motion that is not easily rectified. Ninety-eight percent of injuries seen at rehab centers are human-related.

In recent months, A Place Called Hope has expanded on their private ten acres to two additional sizable eagle aviaries and a hospital made out of an old watershed. Tours, photography events, and presentations are a way for APCH to receive donations and continue to do their excellent work.

For more information about visiting A Place Called Hope or to donate to the raptors, visit aplacecalledhoperaptors.com/rehab.

"Fizzgig," the first-generation eaglet born to our local hometown eagles in New Haven, learning to fly.

Christine Cummings of A Place Called Hope with their resident eagle, Enapi.

Banshee, the resident barn owl at A Place Called Hope. One can sponsor different birds of prey at the rehab facility.

Eshe, the female American kestrel. She lived a long and happy life and was estimated to be eleven or twelve years old. Eshe, meaning life in Swahili, was the epitome of her name and lived eight years with APCH.

Livingston Ripley Waterfowl Conservancy

An additional star in the conservation field is Livingston Ripley Waterfowl Conservancy. The conservancy is home to over eighty species of birds. The institution, founded by S. Dillon Ripley with his entomologist wife, Mary Livingston Ripley, houses 400 birds acquired worldwide. Livingston Ripley aims to educate visitors of all ages in wildlife conservation with hands-on experiences with their waterfowl, wetland habitats, and various programs.

Livingston Ripley also operates as a breeding facility for the genetic diversity of rare and endangered species. Equipped with educators and aviculturists, Ripley has staff who embody passion and leadership in their fields.

Participation with the birds also brings income to support the site. Photography, falconry lessons, and guided tours are a few such ways that the public can support the efforts of the Ripley legacy.

In 2021, Livingston Ripley, in conjunction with DEEP (Department of Energy and Environmental Protection), participated in testing backpack transmitters on captive black ducks. After being attached to ducks in the wild, these transmitters will track the saddled waterfowl's movements telling monitoring biologists about the birds' breeding grounds, nesting, and reproductive rates, giving more insight on how to help increase species numbers.

Right: A Baer's Pochard, the most endangered duck globally, at Livingston Ripley Waterfowl Conservancy.

Below: A Speckled Eider, frolicking at Livingston Ripley Waterfowl Conservancy. This duck is an Arctic sea duck.

A Smew (drake) at the Livingston Ripley Waterfowl Conservancy is the only living member of the genus Mergellus and is a small diving duck.

A Swinhoe's pheasant, aka the Taiwan Blue pheasant, is endemic to Taiwan.

3

The Outdoors: The Parks, Recreation, and Destination

Connecticut is home to 139 state parks and forests. It requires great effort to maintain these spaces to naturally present themselves to the public. This work relies heavily on volunteers and state park personnel. Wildlife is abundant, and the landscape is a photographer's paradise. Waterfalls, rock climbing, skiing, hiking, and water sports are just some of the activities available at any end of the state. There is something for everyone.

This is a view from the top of Web Mountain in Monroe during autumn.

The Shelton/Derby Dam started the industrial revolution in Shelton.

A community water feature from a spring in the historic Aspetuck neighborhood.

A fall walk along a path in Edgewood Park, New Haven.

A view from the top of Meig's Point bridge platform in Hammonasset State Park, in Madison.

Hiking trails offer spectacular views from any mountaintop.

Old New Gate Prison and Copper Mine in East Granby. Bat walks are on the agenda deep into the copper mine.

A farm view through the golden leaves of autumn. There are more than 5,000 farms in Connecticut.

Swans on a foggy lake at sunrise in Hubbard Park in Meriden.

Gillette Castle State Park in East Haddam. Gillette Castle was once home to Sherlock Holmes, better known as stage actor William Gillette.

A view from the docks at Eagle Landing State Park of Goodspeed Opera House and the bridge at sunset.

A view of West Rock State Park in New Haven from the end of West River Oasis.

A look out into the Long Island Sound from the inlet at the end of Short Beach, Lordship/Stratford.

The walk to Charles Island, Milford, is done by the low tide on a jetty. Water can turn in a second and engulf you in the middle or strand you on the island. Many have died and been swept out to sea, crossing at the wrong time or the supposed right time, as currents can change on a whim.

Here is the view from Charles Island in Milford, where Captain William Kidd buried part of his treasure. Kidd's treasure is still unfound.

A sandcastle competition of family fun on Short Beach in Stratford.

Tall ships in the harbor of Mystic, Connecticut.

Fort Trumbull in New London. This representation of the fort was built in 1839 and 1852.

A lone fisherman on a foggy Uncas Lake in Nehantic State Forest. Fishing or boating is also an excellent way to see 5,062 acres of forest from an alternative view.

Connecticut's Steam Locomotive is located in Essex and offers rides seasonally. The scene with Indy's (Harrison Ford) train arrival from *Indiana Jones and the Kingdom of the Crystal Skull* was filmed on our famed steam train.

A river's movement inspired the architecture of Grace Farm's building in New Canaan. Grace Farms is a community center and nature preserve housing a library and tea house.

The fountain from the gardens of Harkness Memorial State Park in Waterford. Harkness is comprised of a mansion and gardens set on 250 acres looking out on the Long Island Sound.

The Lover's Leap Bridge casting late-day shadows from the sun in New Milford.

Valley Forge Gorge/Falls in Weston offers stunning sites and hikes. Connecticut has nineteen recognized waterfalls by a waterfall trail and many others to discover.

A porcupine gives a good scratch on the side of the road in Colebrook. The park systems in this area offer porcupine walks to see these amazing creatures in person.

A double rainbow above Parmalee Farm in Killingworth. Parmalee Farm offers community garden plots, trails for hiking, sugar house tours and instruction, artisan markets, classic car shows and concerts, Halloween pumpkin carving, and more.

Lavender Pond Farm is a fragrant and wondrous place in Killingworth. The farm also offers lavender products and plants from the gift shop—yoga in the lavender fields, photography landscape, a purple train, and a lavender doodle dog mascot.

The sound view from the decimated Shakespeare Playhouse in Stratford. It was once a thriving show space where top acts from the 1950s through the 1970s shined. However, it was ravaged by fire but left a scenic park in its place.

Shown are miniature horse or pony carts at Hammonassett State Park. A pony can pull up to 800 pounds. Pony cart clubs have competitions to do obstacle courses, and Hammonassett offers them wide open spaces to practice.

Dog cart practice at Hammonassett State Park. Also using the grounds for training at Hammo are the dog carters. Draft dog competitors encompass all types of dogs: Bernese Mountain, Saint Bernards, Newfoundlands, and Leonbergers, to name a few.

Classic car shows are looked forward to yearly at the Stratford Municipal Airport.

A skate park across from West Haven, Connecticut beaches also provides BMX recreation and a skate and BMX festival.

4

The Lighthouses

Lighthouses dot the shoreline of Connecticut, facing off against the Long Island Sound. Fourteen active lighthouses line the state's coast; six are inactive, and two are private. Only one structure met the fate of destruction after deactivation. The lights range in height from thirty-one feet to New London's Harbor Light at eighty-nine feet (the tallest). All are uniquely beautiful and set against an enchanting backdrop of the sea.

Connecticut lighthouses featured in numerous stories fail to rival the famous legend of the ghost of the New London Ledge. Coast Guard crews and their visitors often detail knocking, doors opening and closing, and the sheets from their beds being removed. Ernie was probably not the actual name of the lightkeeper from the twenties, but it is the one given to the ghost whose footsteps roam the halls and whose voice calls coast guard service members' names while others sleep. As for the townies report, Ernie's spirit attribution is due to matters of the heart. While tending to his lighthouse duties, Ernie's wife ran off with the Captain of the Block Island Ferry. The loneliness crept in, the grief was overwhelming, and in his melancholy, Ernie climbed to the top of the Ledge Light and plunged to the turbulent and icy depths below. Ernie's body, never recovered, contributes to claims of feeling his presence. Visiting women have claimed to see a ghost, but no other male occupant has. Ernie likes to be helpful, possibly feeling comradery with fellow lightkeepers, and does chores. Some of these chores are cleaning windows and polishing the brass. Of all the poltergeist you could get, I imagine a helpful one is pretty rare and welcomed. The stories are so convincing that the Ledge Light became featured on *Ghost Hunters* and shows like the *Scariest Places on Earth*.

Not all the lights have hauntings or stories, and some are even privately owned, like the New London Harbor Light. The New London Harbor Light, also known to locals as the Pequot Avenue Light, is the tallest lighthouse in Connecticut. The building hosts a museum inside the lighthouse by appointment only. At least this was the regimen before Covid-19 policies.

Make it a goal to map out and see all of them, as each one has unique attributes.

The Avery Point Lighthouse in Groton, Connecticut, is located on the UConn campus. The lighthouse was built in 1943, is forty-three feet high, and is octagonal. The lighthouse's design has Colonial Revival elements, and the designers were Alfred Hopkins and Associates.

An inside shot of the Avery Point Lighthouse.

The Black Rock Harbor Light (aka Fayerweather Light) at sunset in Fayeweather Island, Bridgeport. The light is forty-one feet high and in the Seaside Park Historic District.

The Lighthouse Point Lighthouse in New Haven during the blood moon rising.

Right: The Lighthouse Point Lighthouse on a blustery day. The lighthouse is ninety-seven feet above sea level and was built in 1847.

Below: The New London Ledge Lighthouse is in Groton, Connecticut, and on the mouth of the Thames River. The Ledge light is fifty-eight feet high and was built in 1909.

The New London Harbor Lighthouse was built in 1760 and is the tallest lighthouse at eighty-nine feet in Connecticut.

The Southwest Ledge or New Haven Breakwater Lighthouse was built in 1876 and is forty-five feet tall.

The Old Saybrook Lynde Point Lighthouse was first lit in 1839 and has a focal point of seventy-one feet.

The Stratford Point Lighthouse at night from the grounds of the Stratford Point Audubon.

5

The Landmarks

Yale's Harkness tower looms 216 feet over New Haven; gigantic frog sculptures in various holiday get-ups welcomes you across the bridge into Willimantic, while multiple tall ships dock the piers at many waterfront towns, most commonly Mystic's Harbor. Church spires define the skyline of Newtown from Castle Hill Road. Remnants of the Gasoline Highway, one of the great neon highways of the United States, leave motels like the Hi-Ho on Merritt Parkway as a slow reminder of what progress can do to a town. Distinct and quirky landmarks mark the cities of the nutmeg state.

The Beehive Bridge in New Britain was built to give a new and inviting look through its honeycombs of the city. The bridge's address is Route 72 on the Main Street overpass.

A look from the hive of the Beehive Bridge in New Britain.

The vintage 1960s motel Hi-Ho off the Merrit Parkway in Fairfield has turned on its red neon sign again. The motel has resurfaced as a swanky boutique hotel with a cocktail bar and Barcelona eatery.

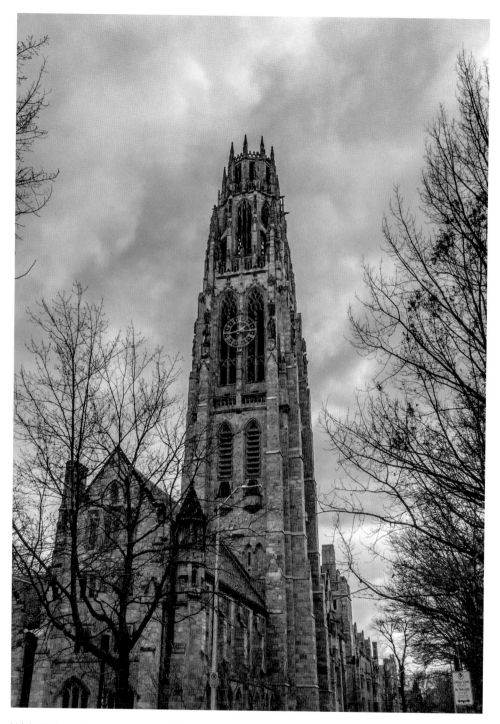

Yale's Harkness Tower on a typical New England Day. Harkness was the first crown tower built-in English Perpendicular Gothic style and is 216 feet tall. The building was an addition to the Memorial Quadrangle donated by Anna M. Harkness to honor her deceased son, Charles William Harkness. Charles was an 1883 Yale graduate.

Yale rooftops through the fall foliage.

Eagle figurehead on the front of the USCGC *Eagle* tall ship.

The USCGC *Eagle* tall ship docked at Fort Trumble on the Thames River.

The Heublin Tower at Talcott Mountain State Park. Heublin is 165 feet tall of Bavarian influence construction. The original owner's fortune was derived from steak sauce and vodka. It is now inevitable for you to think of A1 when viewing it. The grounds provide hiking and biking trails to visitors of this Simsbury attraction.

Above: The view of Newtown on a foggy morning from Castle Hill Road Park. The spires shown are the Newtown Congregational Church and the Trinity Episcopal Church.

Right: Frogs on thread spools will welcome you across the Willimantic Bridge by South Street across the Willimantic River. The Frog Bridge or Thread City Bridge was built in 1857 and was named for the Battle of the Frogs, where residents awoken by bullfrogs mistook their croaks as war drums. The four frogs of the bridge are Manny, Willy, Windy, and Swifty.

47

Covered Bridge at the Devil's Hopyard in East Haddam. Devil's Hopyard is a 1,000-acre state park home to Chapman Falls.

Bull's Bridge. This wooden single-lane vehicular-covered bridge that crosses the Housatonic River was opened in 1842 and is located in Kent.

The Derby-Shelton bridge, or so nicknamed "the three bridges," is a connection between the towns of Derby and Shelton. The bridge was built in 1918, replaces a wooden and covered bridge, and is 469.5 feet across the Housatonic River.

Shelton train bridge from the 1800s in the snow.

6

The Art

Vibrant and alive, the towns of Connecticut showcase their culture, express their feelings, and scream talent from the rooftops. Everyone has a little something to contribute to fascinate the eye and tickle the senses, from culinary to color. Before Covid-19, towns were bursting with art shows and festivals. Old armories in New Haven were turned, room for room, with artists' creations. Parks are lined with tents of creators selling their wares. Here we take a look at art born or housed in our state.

A polar bear sculpture made by graffiti artist "Refractualism" (Instagram name) The bear is made from reclaimed wood and metal from the defunct building where it resides. Metal was nailed and smashed together and then sprayed with a fire extinguisher for color. The artist said there was nothing to paint out there, "so this is what happens." Pretty stellar outcome.

Kismet, when something works. The colorful graffiti and tagging seem to work as one piece even though they are not. The art is inside an old train track tower.

The Hi Crew Goonies graffiti wall in New Haven. The Hi Crew are known for their imaginative and precise talent throughout the Connecticut area. The group is often asked to add art to the greater New Haven area and beyond.

I would consider New London an art town. There are original pieces throughout the downtown area, and they are plentiful. Mural walks are conducted to tour historic downtown and see the sixteen sum murals, drawings, and other installations.

Peter Busby's wire horse sculpture in front of the Brookfield Town Hall.

Elephant topiary in front of an elegant home in Madison.

Trackside Pizzaria in Wallingford is just that, trackside. A pizza joint inside a 1920s Philadelphia subway car sitting next to the train tracks serves up traditional brick oven New Haven-style pizza. What an artful and creative way to serve up a dish.

Lobster Landing in Clinton is how everyone's mental picture of a New England lobster roll joint should look. The landing is also said to have the best lobster rolls in Connecticut. I suggest you try them all and let us know!

Open-air art staggers the grounds of the UConn campus in Groton.

Kinetic art in the parking lot of Hamden Plaza in Hamden. The David Bermant foundation has been responsible for placing his collections of work directly in front of audiences. There used to be buried cars beneath asphalt called the "Ghost Parking Lot" in the plaza's front parking area, but that installation is long gone. All that remains is the whirlygig's constant motion inviting you in to shop and witness the art.

The Morgan Great Hall of the Wadsworth Atheneum in Hartford, Connecticut, houses American and European paintings.

A mummy and its sarcophagus dating the Ptolemaic period of Egyptian History is about 2,300 years old and displayed at the Peabody Museum in New Haven.

7

The Graves

Holding the title of the fifth oldest state means having to bury the dead for much longer. The oldest grave in the archives shows its documented interment in 1644. Notably, graves of today cannot hold a candle to the artful beauty of the sculptured markers and poetry preserved in our state's boneyards for centuries.

In Durham, mystery and mourning become countered with humor and payback on homemade tombstones and granite. Here is an example describing the tale of Mrs. Miller by her estranged son-in-law, who was a tad bent after she supported her daughter's divorce from him:

> Here lies the body of Mrs. Miller,
> Sound asleep on her pillow;
> She was Alonzo Miller's wife.
> She raised the devil all her life.
> The Baptist folks they tolled the bell,
> To tell Old Nick she was coming to hell;
> Old Nick, he swore, and his imps did squall
> "Don't let her in; she will kill us all!"

Mostly the local cemeteries are shrouded in mysterious obelisks, hauntings, or misfit celebrities.

P. T. Barnum, buried in Mount Grove Cemetery in Bridgeport, has a fairly demur marker considering what a big show he was in life. The biggest showman on earth lays beneath a seemingly ordinary tribute.

P. T. Barnum, creator of the "Greatest show on earth!" headstone at Mount Grove Cemetery in Bridgeport.

Above: St. Lawrence Cemetery, seemingly quiet by the nearby bustling city. St. Lawrence is across from Yale Bowl off Route 34. This image was shot in the early morning fog and snow of winter.

Left: The mourning lady drapes across a headstone in Bridgeport's Mount Grove Cemetery.

Tom Thumb

Tom Thumb, aka Colonel Tom Thumb, Barnum's dwarf sideshow act, is buried a stone's throw away from Barnum. P. T. purchased a life-sized statue of Tom and placed it as his gravestone. This act purely represents the eternal bond of these two men. The one seen here is a replica of the original, purchased by the Barnum Festival Society and Mountain Grove Cemetery Association as vandals destroyed the first version. At his death, Colonel Tom Thumb was two feet and eleven inches. Unlike Tom, who was at a starting height of twenty-five inches, playing Cupid or Napoleon on stage, to growing only six inches in his entire lifetime, Colonel Tom Thumb's tombstone "towers" above his final resting place.

Tom Thumb's gravesite at Mount Grove Cemetery Bridgeport.

Watson J. Miller

In Connecticut, a heavy masonic presence resides as it also does in its graveyards. The Old Charges of Freemasonry claim Egypt as the birthplace of the art of masonry. Obelisks equating to a ray of light, eternal life, a symbol of the Egyptian sun god Ra, pervade many New England burial grounds. Some, however, would take it a step further. The grave of Watson J. Miller is a fine example of creating a grand memoriam. A thirty-second-degree mason, Miller would have held the title "Sublime Prince of the Royal Secret." He left instruction to erect a statue of himself on a throne and to this day remains guarded by two sphinxes, the incarnations of royal power, and protectors of temple doors.

Colonel Watson J. Miller's shrine, complete with a Sphinx, in Riverside Cemetery in Shelton.

Center Church Crypt

The Crypt in Center Church at New Haven on the Green represents people buried underground twice. The town erected a devotees meeting house over a portion of the burial ground in 1812-1814. The ground's stones and remains were left intact in their original positions to be protected by the new church's foundation. The enclosed chamber, referenced as "the crypt," was created. One hundred thirty-seven headstones are deteriorating between these walls. Some stones are from the founders of New Haven; other examples are the first wife of Benedict Arnold or President Rutherford Hayes' family. High watermarks outline the grave markers that sat against the wall, contributing, with time, to the acceleration in decay. Restoration is in order.

A panoramic view of the very humid and dimly lit crypt of Center Church on the Green in New Haven.

The outline of worn headstones against the wall in the crypt at Center Church on the Green. Age, moisture, and mold made the tombstone's shape this prominent.

Stone at the crypt at Center Church on the Green. Notice the off-center left alignment of the old stone.

Mary E. Hart

The most famous of the state's graves is Mary E. Hart, more commonly known as Midnight Mary. In 1872, Mary, rumored buried alive, still resides in New Haven's Evergreen Cemetery. Dropping to the floor at midnight, her family, believing her dead, had her buried. Urban legend tells it that Mary's aunt, through a nightmare, felt Mary had not departed. The aunt, being very convincing, had the family dig up their daughter's body. Exhuming the body and upon opening the coffin, her relatives found Mary, petrified in death and fear, with bloody hands and nails. There were scratch marks on the inside lid of the casket.

Mary's gravestone's epitaph offers a foreboding warning: "The people shall be troubled at midnight and pass away." It is believed anybody caught in the graveyard after midnight or who would desecrate her grave would die shortly after.

Offerings often left upon her stone are for "favors." Strange goings-on reported from the neighborhood, the general manager, and passers-by are not uncommon. Strangers gave a lady a ride to her home on Winthrop Avenue, only to find she had disappeared like so many hitchhiker ghost stories. Other rumors are of witchcraft, and that Mary hated the world so much for being buried alive that she walks the yard, taking souls that dare enter past the midnight hour.

Midnight Mary's unremarkable stone with offerings on her grave.

There is a tale about someone dying in Evergreen during a drunken night, but there is a lack of proof to back up the story. Where is the evidence? Is it the bodies floating in the West River, directly across the street? A nude man walked into the graveyard's pond, submerged, and was not seen again until the fire department removed his corpse. Another person was reportedly hanging from the neck in the nearby tree between plots. All instances are available by public record. Perhaps Mary is not just a legend after all.

Sarah Winchester

Another famous lady of Evergreen Cemetery is Sarah Winchester. Sarah was the widow of William Winchester, founder of the Winchester Repeating Arms Company. Sarah is renowned in her own right, not as just the widow of a millionaire but as the builder of the Winchester Mansion, aka Winchester Mystery House, in San Jose, California. The Winchester Mystery House quickly became a tourist attraction with vast, never-ending construction, hallways, winding dead-end corridors, staircases that lead to nowhere, and doors that open to walls or sudden drops. The house is most famous for its hauntings.

At her death, Mary had initially been interred in Alta Mesa Cemetery but was eventually transferred to Evergreen, as it was discovered this was her wish per written request. Mary's intent to be laid to rest with her husband and infant daughter was fulfilled. The request, outlined in her handwritten will, had thirteen parts, all signed thirteen times, undoubtedly due to her belief that she was cursed. Visitors find Sarah's grave a destination just like the Winchester Mystery House. Black veils and flowers lie across her stone with other gifts from her many fans.

Hugh Lofting

Hugh Lofting lies quietly in the back corner of an unsuspecting graveyard in Killingworth, not far from where he lived for the majority of his life. In that house, he spent countless hours writing the adored children's book series, *Dr. Doolittle*. Dr. Doolittle was an English doctor who treated animals instead of humans. In addition to the love and care Doolittle provided to the various animals, he could also speak directly to them in their languages. The stories derived from Hugh's enduring love of animals stemmed from a young age. Lofting died in Santa Monica, California, but lay in Evergreen Cemetery in Killingworth.

Right: Sarah Winchester's headstone, the inspiration for the movie *Winchester,* played by Helen Mirren, is buried alongside her husband and baby daughter in Evergreen Cemetery in New Haven, CT.

Below: Hugh Lofting's humble stone in Killingworth. The Latin inscription means "who will separate us."

Duffy

The ideal gravesite for the perfect boy lies looking out across the Connecticut River and Long Island Sound at Avery Point in Groton. The grave of Duffy, the USCG mascot, is that place. Duffy was a stray that wandered into the hearts and lives of the U.S. Coast Guard's security detachment. He lived with twenty security team members, had his table place settings and meals prepared, and even had a tailored uniform so he could march with the rest of the guys. Duffy was well-loved in life and death. A scruffy, rugged bulldog mix received a lifetime of love and gave it in return.

Duffy's (the United States Coast Guard's mascot) grave at UConn in Groton.

8

The Quaint

Thanks to *Gilmore Girls*, Connecticut will never outlive the quaint stereotype. Nor should it. Though admittedly, we are not set all the time in autumn, with multi-colored leaves gently falling at our feet and children running down the jack-o-lantern laden sidewalks in their fuzzy bear costumes. Honestly, it sometimes feels like that scenario off the right road and down specific paths. There is not enough time to document all the flawlessly charming situations one might find from one end of the state to the other, but here are a few to enjoy.

An old dairy farm's barns turned home and studio in Redding.

Strawberry Hollow Farm is the epitome of quaint New England Halloween. You can go to them for your fall mums and pumpkins while also viewing the spectacle of their giant pumpkins for fair competitions. The shops offer holiday-inspired gifts for Halloween and Christmas. Strawberry Hollow Farm calls Guilford it's home.

The dam at the gristmill at sunset in historic Aspetuck Village in Easton.

A Connecticut staple is apple picking at Bishop's Orchards in the fall. Please make your way into their supple farm stand when you are done in the orchard. Bishops also have a line of wines hailing out of Guilford.

Gloria, a ramshackle old houseboat, sits amongst the geese and egrets across from the Inn at Longshore and golf course in Westport.

A yurt sits snuggly in the depth of the Killingworth woods.

Downtown Colebrook's oldest surviving house, the Samuel Rockwell House.

Hacienda Polska's Tree of Life Barn Quilt block is one of nineteen quilt blocks on the Quilt Block Trail of New Milford.

A pristine horse barn in the snow, somewhere out there in Connecticut.

A garage barn withstands a white-out blizzard in Weston.

A summer boat cottage on a pond in Killingworth.

Main Street Durham showing their Halloween flair.

A classic ragtop convertible sits against the backdrop of the once Killingworth Café in Killingworth.

Crepes Choupette gave us a taste of France from its cart in front of the Yale Museum. The flowered bicycle cart eventually turned into a full-blown restaurant. These are the things of dreams!

A bicycle leans against a window full of French's mustard at the Clinton staple of Clam Castle. Typical New England and delicious.

Nothing says charming quite like cuddling livestock. Bradley Mountain Farm in Southington offers goat cuddles, hot yoga, and holiday photos with your favorite cuddle companions.

Everyone needs a little kindness, and it is easily found at the fountain at Bauer Farm in Madison.

Beech Tree Cottages are booming in the summertime for beach lovers. Their Christmas Shop gives you all the warm fuzzies of a Madison Christmas in winter.

The Children's Center gate speaks volumes of creativity and whimsy for this preschool in New Milford.

9

The Weird, Wild, and Wonderful

All places have their big ball of yarn, and Connecticut is no exception. Roadside America scenarios are abundant from one town border to the other. The characters that create them offer much to our society by letting us ride down the road and see what they offer. Nothing beats the smile a giant red, white, and blue chair provides, shrubbery shaped like elephants, or a raised eyebrow from a porch full of mannequins. Hopefully, you will get the same joyful giggle or emotion seeing these photos as we did when we stopped to take them.

A one-bedroom, one-bath 1,672-square-foot condo in a UFO-inspired complex will cost you around $338,000 in Guilford.

Mannequins pile against the door of a house on a backroad in Connecticut. It's like a zombie invasion trying to get in, just with headless mannequins.

What the truck? The Tonka truck tree in Redding is a memorial set up by his artist father, who lost his son. It brings joy to many passersby.

Beaumont Farm in Wallingford often sets up holiday-themed scenarios for the kids (and adults alike). For Christmas one year, we were treated to *Christmas Vacation* scenarios.

The Cushing Center is an archival collection of over 2,200 case studies involving the brain. The center is located on the Yale University Campus in New Haven.

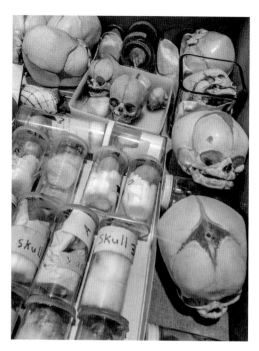

Above left: A child's articulated skeleton at the Cushing Center in New Haven.

Above right: Children's skulls in a drawer of the Cushing Center at Yale University.

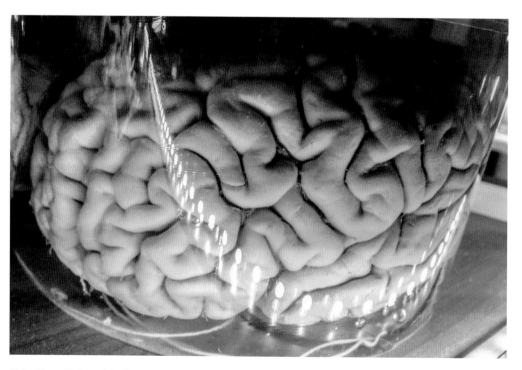

Abby Normal? One of the brains in a jar at the Cushing Center.

The Witch's Dungeon Classic Movie Museum in Bristol houses wax figures of the greats of classic horror movies. These wax sculptures are from *The Mummy*, a film with Boris Karloff disguised as a modern Egyptian named Ardeth Bay. The premise is that Imhotep is searching for his lost love, whom he believes has been reincarnated into a modern girl.

A shot of the wax mummy and its sarcophagus at the Witch's Dungeon Museum.

Vincent Price, the prince of horror, in wax at the Witch's Dungeon in Bristol.

"Powerful you have become, the dark side I sense in you." – Yoda

St. Margaret's Shrine in Bridgeport reminds one of a New Mexico graveyard or grotto. Roadside America calls it a Vatican knockoff.

Prayer candles line the rocky shrine at sunset in St. Margarets in Bridgeport.

The Pez Museum in Orange has an eclectic collection of Pez dispensers. Space Ray guns were some of my favorites, and I am always looking for some.

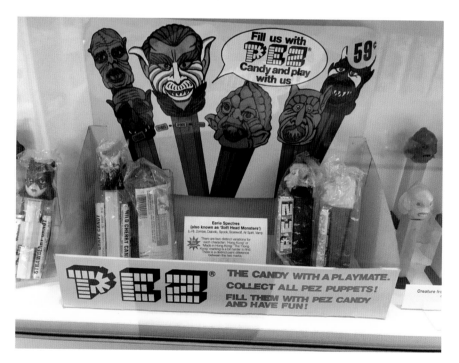

The Pez classic horror dispenser pack is incased at the Pez Museum in Orange.

Gigantic Legos outside the Lego Headquarters in Enfield.

We found bigfoot at Bohemian Pizza and Tacos in Litchfield.

A marker for the unborn turtles we lost at Milford. Please bow your heads.

Stowes, a privately owned seafood restaurant in West Haven, helps feed you and sends you on your way to look for pirate booty on Charles Island. The restaurant is pirate-themed inside and out and offers some of the best chowders around.

The eagle's nest at the Harry C. Barnes Nature Center is fun for kids and grown-ups, too.

A metal sculpture praying mantis reads *Lord of the Flies* to the neighborhood at the Old Saybrook Library.

A metal Xenomorph-like sculpture stands menacingly outside the package store in Branford.

The Easter Island statue stands outside the defunct Timex Museum in Waterbury.

Guilford's puppy mailbox was initially for a recently defunct veterinarian's office but is now the mailbox of a package store.

The fountain at this Clinton antique store freezes every year, giving people something to look at or exclaim in horror how the owner is going to bust his fountain. Either way, it's pretty cool.

A burlap sack of Santaria is exposed at West River Park in New Haven.

A closer look at the Saks contents includes chicken feathers, candles, coins, vegetables, fruit, and pieces of clothing.

Right: A hoodoo spell is uncovered in Evergreen Cemetery under the weeping willow tree by the pond in New Haven.

Below: Eagle Rock was a frog before transforming into a bird in Amston. Don't worry; we have a turtle on the way to Hammonassett in Madison as well.

A toothy grin from our dragon buddy at Bohemian Pizza and Tacos in Litchfield.

A white elephant on the front lawn of a beach house in Milford. It resembles an elephant from the Disney film *The Sorcerer's Apprentice*.

A dime store Indian still represents a convenience store and tobacco location at the Shamrock in Killingworth.

The big patriotic chair in a home's yard entering Killingworth. It gives you the *Alice in Wonderland* vibe of one pill, making you smaller. I often wonder: Do they want someone to come and sit in it?

Bibliography

Hopkins, A., The Patch "Lost and Forgotten: Sunrise Resort," patch.com/connecticut/thehaddams-killingworth/bp--lost-and-forgotten-sunrise-resort

A Place Called Hope, Birds of Prey Rehabilitation Center, aplacecalledhoperaptors.com

Anton Forest Organization, atonforest.org

Bohemian Pizza and Tacos, bohemianpizzaandtacos.com

Bradley Mountain Farm, Goat Cuddle Therapy, bradleymountainfarm.com

British Art Yale Education, Yale Center for British Art, britishart.yale.edu

Center Church on the Green, The Crypt, centerchurchonthegreen.org/history/crypt

Clam Castle CT, clamcastlect.com

Clinton Antique Center Connecticut, clintonantiquecenterct.com

C.T. Gov DEEP, State Parks, Fort Trumball State Park, portal.ct.gov/DEEP/State-Parks/Parks/Fort-Trumbull-State-Park

C.T. Department of Transportation, CT State Gov, portal.ct.gov/dot

C.T. Portal State Governments, State Parks, portal.ct.gov/DEEP/State-Parks

Dinosaur State Park, dinosaurstatepark.org

Dooling, M., *An Historical Account of Charles Island* (Milford, CT: The Carrollton Press, 2006)

Fairfield County National Register of Historic Places, nationalregisterofhistoricplaces.com/ct/fairfield/state

Friends of the Heublein Tower Organization, Heublein Tower History, friendsofheubleintower.org/about-the-heublein-tower

Goodspeed Organization, goodspeed.org

Go Skate, Skate Park: West Haven, goskate.com

Grace Farms Organization, gracefarms.org/grace-farms-foundation

Hladky, G., "Sandy Hooks Uncertain Legacy," *Hartford Courant* (Sandy Hook, CT: 2015)

Hotel Hi-Ho, www.hotelhiho.com

Lavender Pond Farm, www.lavenderpondfarm.com

Lerner, J., "Midnight Mary Continues to Haunt Evergreen Cemetery," *New Haven Register* (New Haven, CT: 2021)

Living Places, Colebrook Center Historic District, livingplaces.com/CT/Litchfield_County/ Colebrook_Town/Colebrook_Center_Historic_District

Lobster Landing, LLC, facebook.com/LobsterLandingLLC

Monroe County Parks and Recreation Department, Webb Mountain Park, monroerec. org/info

National Register of Historic Places, "American Thread Company," ahs-inc.biz/legacy/ pawcatuck/NR-Nomination.pdf

Nature's Art Village, The Dinosaur Place, naturesartvillage.com/experience/the-dinosaur-place

New England Lighthouses; A Virtual Guide, Web Archives, newenglandlighthouses.net

New England Waterfalls, Valley Forge Falls, newenglandwaterfalls.com

Nyberg, A., French Chef in New Haven Upgrades food cart to his own crepe restaurant, wtnh.com/on-air/nyberg/ french-chef-in-new-haven-upgrades-food-cart-to-his-own-crepe-restaurant

Nyberg, A., Yep, Lego's North American Headquarters is in Connecticut, networkconnecticut. com/2015/04/yep-legos-north-america-headquarters-is-in-connecticut

Ousatonic Water Power Company; Dam and Canals, "Historic American Engineering Record," loc.gov/item/ct0426

Payne, Brigham, "The Battle of the Frogs" in *The Story of Bacchus and Centennial Souvenir* (Hartford, CT: A.E. Brooks, 1876)

Peabody Museum of Natural History, peabody.yale.edu

Philips, D., "Legends of Pirate Gold" in *Legendary Connecticut* (Milford, CT: Curbstone Press, 2001)

Ripley Waterfowl Conservancy Organization, ripleyconservancy.org

Roadside America, Eagle Rock, roadsideamerica.com/tip/3449

Roadside America, Timex Museum and Easter Island Statue, roadsideamerica.com/ tip/4509

Roadside America, Bridgeport Vatican Gardens Knockoff, roadsideamerica.com/tip/2414

Rogak, L., *Stones and Bones of New England: A Guide to Unusual, Historic, and Otherwise Notable Cemeteries* (Globe Pequat, 2004)

Santiago, E., "Tall Ship Barque Eagle Sails Into Home Port New London Thursday," *The Patch*, patch.com/connecticut/newlondon/ tall-ship-barque-eagle-sails-homeport-new-london-thursday

Shkolnik, D., "Hi-Crew New Haven – When the Wall Came Down," *Ink Magazine* (New Haven, CT: 2021)

Short Escapes, "USA / New England, Newtown, CT.," shortescapes.net/escape/4039735/ a-literary-landscape-newtown-ct/content/2

Stacom, D., "Beehive Bridge Giving a New Look to New Britain," Hartford Courant, courant.com/community/new-britain/hc-news-new-britain-beehive-bridge

Stowes Food CT, stowesseafoodct.com

Strawberry Hollow Farm, facebook.com/pages/category/Farm/Strawberry-Hollow-Farm-122166581174910

The Connecticut History Organization, chs.org

The Cushing Center, Yale Library Medicine Education, library.medicine.yale.edu/cushingcenter

The Paper Tyger Blogspot, The Stallion, Foal and Mare, thepapertyger.blogspot.com

The Town of Colebrook Organization, townofcolebrook.org

Trackside Pizzeria, tracksidepizzeria.com

US Pez, us.pez.com

Watson, J. Miller, P.T. Barnum, Tom Thumb, Midnight Mary, Find A Grave, findagrave.com

Williams, S., "The Harkness Memorial Tower," American Architect

Coffey, B., "New Sculptures Enliven Outside Spaces at Old Saybrook's Acton Library," shorepublishing.com/news/20150811/new-sculptures-enliven-outside-spaces-at-old-saybrookx2019s-acton-library